DATE DUE

GAYLORD			PRINTED IN U.S.A

THE NONSENSE POEMS OF EDWARD LEAR

THE NONSENSE POEMS OF EDWARD LEAR

Illustrated by Leslie Brooke

Clarion Books
a Houghton Mifflin Company imprint
215 Park Avenue South, New York, NY 10003

An Albion Book
Designer: Andrew Shoolbred

Typesetting and color origination by York House, London
Printed and bound in Hong Kong by South China Printing Co.

Library of Congress Cataloging-in-Publication Data

Lear, Edward, 1812-1888.
    The nonsense poems of Edward Lear/illustrated by Leslie Brooke.
      p.   cm.
    Summary: A collection of nonsense poems by Edward Lear,
illustrated by Leslie Brooke, one of the most popular illustrators
of the early twentieth century.
    ISBN 0-395-57001-8
    1. Nonsense verses, English. 2. Children's poetry, English.
[1. Nonsense verses. 2. English poetry.] I. Brooke, L. Leslie
(Leonard Leslie), 1862-1940, ill. II. Title.
PR4879.L2A6 1991   90-42354
821'.8--dc20   CIP
                                               AC

00 10 9 8 7 6 5 4 3 2 1

Contents

The Self-portrait of the Laureate of Nonsense

How pleasant to know Mr Lear!
    Who has written such volumes of stuff!
Some think him ill-tempered and queer,
    But a few think him pleasant enough.

His mind is concrete and fastidious,
    His nose is remarkably big;
His visage is more or less hideous,
    His beard it resembles a wig.

He has ears, and two eyes, and ten fingers,
    Leastways if you reckon two thumbs;
Long ago he was one of the singers,
    But now he is one of the dumbs.

He sits in a beautiful parlour,
    With hundreds of books on the wall;
He drinks a great deal of Marsala,
    But never gets tipsy at all.

He has many friends, laymen and clerical;
    Old Foss is the name of his cat;
His body is perfectly spherical,
    He weareth a runcible hat.

When he walks in a waterproof white,
   The children run after him so!
Calling out, "He's come out in his night-
   Gown, that crazy old Englishman, oh!"

He weeps by the side of the ocean,
   He weeps on the top of the hill;
He purchases pancakes and lotion,
   And chocolate shrimps from the mill.

He reads but he cannot speak Spanish,
   He cannot abide ginger-beer:
Ere the days of his pilgrimage vanish,
   How pleasant to know Mr Lear!

The Owl and the Pussy-cat went to sea
   In a beautiful pea-green boat,
They took some honey, and plenty of money,
   Wrapped up in a five-pound note.
The Owl looked up to the stars above,
   And sang to a small guitar,
"O lovely Pussy! O Pussy, my love,
    What a beautiful Pussy you are,
      You are,
      You are!
   What a beautiful Pussy you are!"

Pussy said to the Owl, "You elegant fowl!
　　How charmingly sweet you sing!
O let us be married! Too long we have tarried:
　　But what shall we do for a ring?"
They sailed away, for a year and a day,
　　To the land where the Bong-tree grows
And there in a wood a Piggy-wig stood
　　With a ring at the end of his nose,
　　　　　His nose,
　　　　　His nose,
　　With a ring at the end of his nose.

"Dear Pig, are you willing to sell for one shilling
    Your ring?" Said the Piggy, "I will."
So they took it away, and were married next day
    By the Turkey who lives on the hill.
They dined on mince, and slices of quince,
    Which they ate with a runcible spoon;
And hand in hand, on the edge of the sand,
    They danced by the light of the moon,
        The moon,
        The moon,
    They danced by the light of the moon.

When awful darkness and silence reign
Over the great Gromboolian plain,
    Through the long, long wintry nights; –
When the angry breakers roar
As they beat on the rocky shore; –
    When Storm-clouds brood on the towering heights
Of the Hills of the Chankly Bore: –

Then, through the vast and gloomy dark,
There moves what seems a fiery spark,
    A lonely spark with silvery rays
    Piercing the coal-black night, –
    A Meteor strange and bright: –
Hither and thither the vision strays,
    A single lurid light.

Slowly it wanders, – pauses, – creeps, –
Anon it sparkles, – flashes and leaps;
And ever as onward it gleaming goes
A light on the Bong-tree stems it throws.
And those who watch at that midnight hour
From Hall or Terrace, or lofty Tower,
Cry, as the wild light passes along, –
        "The Dong! – the Dong!
    The wandering Dong through the forest goes!
        The Dong! the Dong!
    The Dong with a luminous Nose!"

Long years ago
The Dong was happy and gay,
Till he fell in love with a Jumbly Girl
Who came to those shores one day,
For the Jumblies came in a Sieve, they did, –
Landing at eve near the Zemmery Fidd
Where the Oblong Oysters grow,
And the rocks are smooth and gray.
And all the woods and the valleys rang
With the Chorus they daily and nightly sang, –

"Far and few, far and few,
Are the lands where the Jumblies live;
Their heads are green, and their hands are blue
And they went to sea in a Sieve."

Happily, happily passed those days!
    While the cheerful Jumblies staid;
  They danced in circlets all night long,
  To the plaintive pipe of the lively Dong,
    In moonlight, shine, or shade.
For day and night he was always there
By the side of the Jumbly Girl so fair,
With her sky-blue hands, and her sea-green hair.
Till the morning came of that hateful day
When the Jumblies sailed in their Sieve away,
And the Dong was left on the cruel shore
Gazing – gazing for evermore, –
Ever keeping his weary eyes on
That pea-green sail on the far horizon, –
Singing the Jumbly Chorus still
As he sate all day on the grassy hill, –
    "Far and few, far and few,
    Are the lands where the Jumblies live;
    Their heads are green, and their hands are blue,
    And they went to sea in a Sieve."

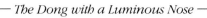

But when the sun was low in the West,
   The Dong arose and said; –
– "What little sense I once possessed
   Has quite gone out of my head!" –

And since that day he wanders still
By lake and forest, marsh and hill,
Singing – "O somewhere, in valley or plain
Might I find my Jumbly Girl again!
For ever I'll seek by lake and shore
Till I find my Jumbly Girl once more!"

Playing a pipe with silvery squeaks,
Since then his Jumbly Girl he seeks,
And because by night he could not see,
He gathered the bark of the Twangum Tree
   On the flowery plain that grows.
   And he wove him a wondrous Nose, –
A Nose as strange as a Nose could be!
Of vast proportions and painted red,
And tied with cords to the back of his head.
      – In a hollow rounded space it ended
     With a luminous Lamp within suspended,
      All fenced about
      With a bandage stout
      To prevent the wind from blowing it out; –
     And with holes all round to send the light,
     In gleaming rays on the dismal night.

And now each night, and all night long,
Over those plains still roams the Dong;
And above the wail of the Chimp and Snipe
You may hear the squeak of his plaintive pipe
While ever he seeks, but seeks in vain
To meet with his Jumbly Girl again;
Lonely and wild – all night he goes, –
The Dong with a luminous Nose!
And all who watch at the midnight hour,
From Hall or Terrace, or lofty Tower,
Cry, as they trace the Meteor bright,
Moving along through the dreary night, –
     "This is the hour when forth he goes,
     The Dong with a luminous Nose!
     Yonder – over the plain he goes;
       He goes!
       He goes;
     The Dong with a luminous Nose!"

CALICO PIE

Calico Pie,
The little Birds fly
Down to the calico tree,
Their wings were blue,
And they sang "Tilly-loo!"
Till away they flew, –
And they never came back to me!
They never came back!
They never came back!
They never came back to me!

Calico Jam,
The little Fish swam,
Over the syllabub sea,
He took off his hat,
To the Sole and the Sprat,
And the Willeby-wat, –
But he never came back to me!
He never came back!
He never came back!
He never came back to me!

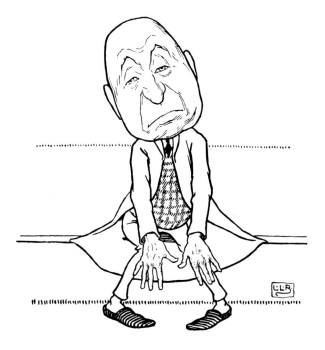

Calico Ban,
  The little Mice ran,
To be ready in time for tea,
  Flippity flup,
  They drank it all up,
  And danced in the cup, –
But they never came back to me!
  They never came back!
  They never came back!
They never came back to me!

Calico Drum,
The Grasshoppers come,
The Butterfly, Beetle, and Bee,
Over the ground,
Around and round,
With a hop and a bound, –
But they never came back!
They never came back!
They never came back!
They never came back to me!

The Pobble who has no toes
    Had once as many as we;
When they said, "Some day you may lose them all;" –
    He replied, – "Fish fiddle de-dee!"
And his Aunt Jobiska made him drink,
Lavender water tinged with pink,
For she said, "The World in general knows
There's nothing so good for a Pobble's toes!"

The Pobble who has no toes,
   Swam across the Bristol Channel;
But before he set out he wrapped his nose,
   In a piece of scarlet flannel.
For his Aunt Jobiska said, "No harm
Can come to his toes if his nose is warm;
And it's perfectly known that a Pobble's toes
Are safe, – provided he minds his nose."

The Pobble swam fast and well
   And when boats or ships came near him
He tinkledy-binkledy-winkled a bell
   So that all the world could hear him.
And all the Sailors and Admirals cried,
When they saw him nearing the further side, –
"He has gone to fish, for his Aunt Jobiska's
Runcible Cat with crimson whiskers!"

But before he touched the shore,
   The shore of the Bristol Channel,
A sea-green Porpoise carried away
   His wrapper of scarlet flannel.
And when he came to observe his feet
Formerly garnished with toes so neat
His face at once became forlorn
On perceiving that all his toes were gone!

And nobody ever knew
   From that dark day to the present,
Whoso had taken the Pobble's toes,
   In a manner so far from pleasant.
Whether the shrimps or crawfish gray,
Or crafty Mermaids stole them away –
Nobody knew; and nobody knows
How the Pobble was robbed of his twice five toes!

The Pobble who has no toes
    Was placed in a friendly Bark,
And they rowed him back, and carried him up,
    To his Aunt Jobiska's Park.
And she made him a feast at his earnest wish
Of eggs and buttercups fried with fish; –
And she said, – "It's a fact the whole world knows,
That Pobbles are happier without their toes."

The Courtship of the Yonghy-Bonghy-Bò

Music by Edward Lear

CANTO.

PIANO.

On the coast of Co - ro - man-del, Where the ear - ly pumpkins grow, In the

middle of the woods, Lived the Yonghy Bonghy Bò; Two old chairs and half a candle, One old

jug with-out a han-dle; These were all his worldly goods, In the middle of the woods, These were

all the world-ly goods, Of the Yong-hy Bong-hy Bò, Of the Yong-hy Bong-hy Bò.

THE COURTSHIP OF THE YONGHY~BONGHY~BO

On the Coast of Coromandel
Where the early pumpkins blow,
In the middle of the woods
   Lived the Yonghy-Bonghy-Bò.
Two old chairs, and half a candle, –
One old jug without a handle, –
     These were all his worldly goods:
     In the middle of the woods,
     These were all the worldly goods,
   Of the Yonghy-Bonghy-Bò.
   Of the Yonghy-Bonghy-Bò.

Once, among the Bong-trees walking
   Where the early pumpkins blow,
     To a little heap of stones
   Came the Yonghy-Bonghy-Bò.
There he heard a Lady talking,
To some milk-white Hens of Dorking, –
     " 'Tis the Lady Jingly Jones!
     On that little heap of stones
     Sits the Lady Jingly Jones!"
   Said the Yonghy-Bonghy-Bò,
   Said the Yonghy-Bonghy-Bò.

"Lady Jingly! Lady Jingly!
   Sitting where the pumpkins blow,
     Will you come and be my wife?"
   Said the Yonghy-Bonghy-Bò.
"I am tired of living singly, –
On this coast so wild and shingly, –
     I'm a-weary of my life:
     If you'll come and be my wife,
     Quite serene would be my life!" –
   Said the Yonghy-Bonghy-Bò,
   Said the Yonghy-Bonghy-Bò.

"On this Coast of Coromandel,
     Shrimps and watercresses grow,
          Prawns are plentiful and cheap,"
     Said the Yonghy-Bonghy-Bò.
"You shall have my chairs and candle,
And my jug without a handle! –
          Gaze upon the rolling deep
          (Fish is plentiful and cheap)
          As the sea, my love is deep!"
     Said the Yonghy-Bonghy-Bò,
     Said the Yonghy-Bonghy-Bò.

Lady Jingly answered sadly,
     And her tears began to flow, –
          "Your proposal comes too late,
     Mr Yonghy-Bonghy-Bò!
I would be your wife most gladly!"
(Here she twirled her fingers madly)
          "But in England I've a mate!
          Yes! you've asked me far too late,
          For in England I've a mate,
     Mr Yonghy-Bonghy-Bò!
     Mr Yonghy-Bonghy-Bò!"

"Mr Jones – (his name is Handel, –
　Handel Jones, Esquire, & Co.)
　　Dorking fowls delights to send,
　Mr Yonghy-Bonghy-Bò!
Keep, oh! keep your chairs and candle,
And your jug without a handle, –
　　I can merely be your friend!
　　– Should my Jones more Dorkings send,
　　I will give you three, my friend!
　Mr Yonghy-Bonghy-Bò!
　Mr Yonghy-Bonghy-Bò!"

"Though you've such a tiny body,
　And your head so large doth grow, –
　　Though your hat may blow away,
　Mr Yonghy-Bonghy-Bò!
Though you're such a Hoddy Doddy –
Yet I wish that I could modi-
　　fy the words I needs must say!
　　Will you please to go away?
　　That is all I have to say –
　Mr Yonghy-Bonghy-Bò!
　Mr Yonghy-Bonghy-Bò!"

Down the slippery slopes of Myrtle,
  Where the early pumpkins blow,
    To the calm and silent sea
  Fled the Yonghy-Bonghy-Bò.
There, beyond the Bay of Gurtle,
Lay a large and lively Turtle; –
    "You're the Cove," he said, "for me
    On your back beyond the sea,
    Turtle, you shall carry me!"
  Said the Yonghy-Bonghy-Bò,
  Said the Yonghy-Bonghy-Bò.

Through the silent-roaring ocean
  Did the Turtle swiftly go;
    Holding fast upon his shell
  Rode the Yonghy-Bonghy-Bò.
With a sad primeval motion
Towards the sunset isles of Boshen
    Still the Turtle bore him well.
    Holding fast upon his shell,
    "Lady Jingly Jones, farewell!"
  Sang the Yonghy-Bonghy-Bò,
  Sang the Yonghy-Bonghy-Bò.

From the Coast of Coromandel,
   Did that Lady never go;
      On that heap of stones she mourns
   For the Yonghy-Bonghy-Bò.
On that Coast of Coromandel,
In his jug without a handle
      Still she weeps, and daily moans;
      On that little heap of stones
      To her Dorking Hens she moans,
   For the Yonghy-Bonghy-Bò,
   For the Yonghy-Bonghy-Bò.

On the top of the Crumpetty Tree
    The Quangle Wangle sat,
But his face you could not see,
    On account of his Beaver Hat.
For his Hat was a hundred and two feet wide,
With ribbons and bibbons on every side
And bells, and buttons, and loops, and lace,
So that nobody ever could see the face
        Of the Quangle Wangle Quee.

The Quangle Wangle said
    To himself on the Crumpetty Tree, –
"Jam; and jelly; and bread;
    Are the best food for me!
But the longer I live on this Crumpetty Tree
The plainer than ever it seems to me
That very few people come this way
And that life on the whole is far from gay!"
        Said the Quangle Wangle Quee.

But there came to the Crumpetty Tree,
    Mr and Mrs Canary;
And they said, – "Did you ever see
    Any spot so charmingly airy?
May we build a nest on your lovely Hat?
Mr Quangle Wangle, grant us that!
O please let us come and build a nest
Of whatever material suits you best,
    Mr Quangle Wangle Quee!"

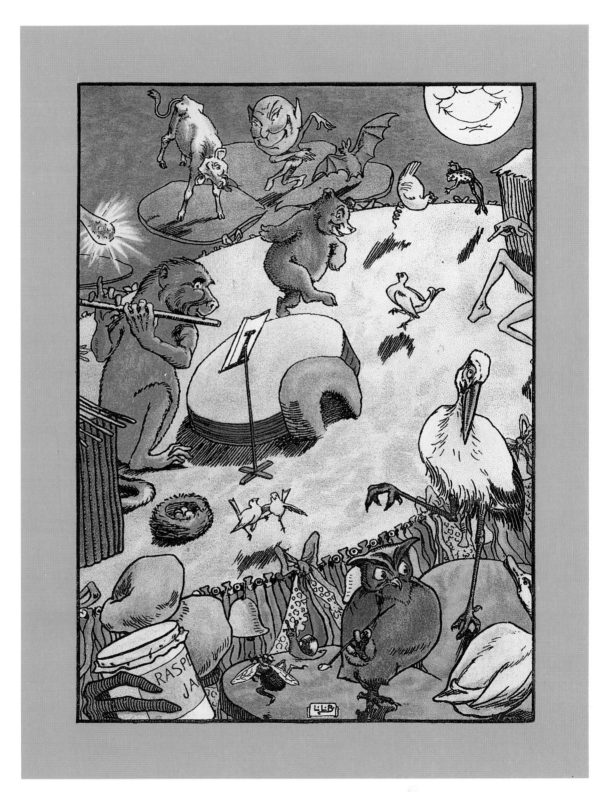

And besides, to the Crumpetty Tree
   Came the Stork, the Duck, and the Owl;
   The Snail, and the Bumble-Bee,
   The Frog, and the Fimble Fowl;
(The Fimble Fowl, with a Corkscrew leg;)
And all of them said, – "We humbly beg,
We may build our homes on your lovely Hat, –
Mr Quangle Wangle, grant us that!
     Mr Quangle Wangle Quee!"

And the Golden Grouse came there,
   And the Pobble who has no toes, –
And the small Olympian bear, –
   And the Dong with a luminous Nose.
And the Blue Baboon, who played the Flute, –
And the Orient Calf from the Land of Tute, –
And the Attery Squash, and the Bisky Bat, –
All came and built on the lovely Hat
     Of the Quangle Wangle Quee.

And the Quangle Wangle said
    To himself on the Crumpetty Tree, –
"When all these creatures move
    What a wonderful noise there'll be!"
And at night by the light of the Mulberry moon
They danced to the Flute of the Blue Baboon,
On the broad green leaves of the Crumpetty Tree,
And all were as happy as happy could be,
    With the Quangle Wangle Quee.

On a little piece of wood,
Mr Spikky Sparrow stood;
Mrs Sparrow sate close by,
A-making of an insect pie,
For her little children five,
In the nest and all alive,
Singing with a cheerful smile
To amuse them all the while
Twikky wikky wikky wee,
Wikky bikky twikky tee,
Spikky bikky bee!

Mrs Spikky Sparrow said,
"Spikky, Darling! In my head
Many thoughts of trouble come,
Like to flies upon a plum!
All last night, among the trees,
I heard you cough, I heard you sneeze;
And, thought I, it's come to that
Because he does not wear a hat!
    Chippy wippy sikky tee!
    Bikky wikky tikky mee!
      Spikky chippy wee!

"Not that you are growing old,
But the nights are growing cold.
No one stays out all night long
Without a hat: I'm sure it's wrong!"
Mr Spikky said, "How kind,
Dear! you are, to speak your mind!
All your life I wish you luck!
You are! You are! a lovely duck!
    Witchy witchy witchy wee!
    Twitchy witchy witchy bee!
      Tikky tikky tee!

"I was also sad, and thinking,
When one day I saw you winking,
And I heard you sniffle-snuffle,
And I saw your feathers ruffle;
To myself I sadly said,
She's neuralgia in her head!
That dear head has nothing on it!
Ought she not to wear a bonnet?
Witchy kitchy kitchy wee?
Spikky wikky mikky bee?
Chippy wippy chee?

"Let us both fly up to town!
There I'll buy you such a gown!
Which, completely in the fashion,
You shall tie a sky-blue sash on.
And a pair of slippers neat,
To fit your darling little feet,
So that you will look and feel
Quite galloobious and genteel!
Jikky wikky bikky see,
Chikky bikky wikky bee,
Twicky witchy wee!"

So they both to London went,
Alighting on the Monument,
Whence they flew down swiftly – pop,
Into Moses' wholesale shop;
There they bought a hat and bonnet,
And a gown with spots upon it,
A satin sash of Cloxam blue,
And a pair of slippers too.
    Zikky wikky mikky bee,
    Witchy witchy mitchy kee,
      Sikky tikky wee.

Then when so completely drest,
Back they flew, and reached their nest.
Their children cried, "O Ma and Pa!
How truly beautiful you are!"
Said they, "We trust that cold or pain
We shall never feel again!
While, perched on tree, or house, or steeple,
We now shall look like other people.
  Witchy witchy witchy wee,
  Twikky mikky bikky bee,
    Zikky sikky tee."

They went to sea in a Sieve, they did,
   In a Sieve they went to sea;
In spite of all their friends could say,
On a winter's morn, on a stormy day,
   In a Sieve they went to sea!
And when the Sieve turned round and round,
And everyone cried, "You'll all be drowned!"
They called aloud, "Our Sieve ain't big,
But we don't care a button! We don't care a fig!
   In a Sieve we'll go to sea!"
    Far and few, far and few,
      Are the lands where the Jumblies live;
      Their heads are green, and their hands are blue,
      And they went to sea in a Sieve.

They sailed away in a Sieve, they did,
   In a Sieve they sailed so fast,
With only a beautiful pea-green veil
Tied with a riband by way of a sail,
   To a small tobacco-pipe mast;
And everyone said, who saw them go,
"O won't they be soon upset, you know!
For the sky is dark, and the voyage is long,
And happen what may, it's extremely wrong
   In a Sieve to sail so fast!"
    Far and few, far and few,
      Are the lands where the Jumblies live;
      Their heads are green, and their hands are blue,
      And they went to sea in a Sieve.

The water it soon came in, it did,
  The water soon came in;
So to keep them dry, they wrapped their feet
In a pinky paper all folded neat,
  And they fastened it down with a pin.
And they passed the night in a crockery-jar,
And each of them said, "How wise we are!

Though the sky be dark, and the voyage be long,
Yet we never can think we were rash or wrong,
   While round in our Sieve we spin!"
      Far and few, far and few,
         Are the lands where the Jumblies live;
      Their heads are green, and their hands are blue,
         And they went to sea in a Sieve.

And all night long they sailed away;
   And when the sun went down,
They whistled and warbled a moony song
To the echoing sound of a coppery gong,
   In the shade of the mountains brown.
"O Timballo! How happy we are,
When we live in a sieve and a crockery-jar,
And all night long in the moonlight pale,
We sail away with a pea-green sail,
   In the shade of the mountains brown!"
      Far and few, far and few,
         Are the lands where the Jumblies live;
      Their heads are green, and their hands are blue,
         And they went to sea in a Sieve.

They sailed to the Western Sea, they did,
　To a land all covered with trees,
And they bought an Owl, and a useful Cart,
And a pound of Rice, and a Cranberry Tart,
　And a hive of silvery Bees.
And they bought a Pig, and some green Jack-daws,
And a lovely Monkey with lollipop paws,
And forty bottles of Ring-Bo-Ree,
　And no end of Stilton Cheese.
　　Far and few, far and few,
　　　Are the lands where the Jumblies live;
　　Their heads are green, and their hands are blue,
　　　And they went to sea in a Sieve.

And in twenty years they all came back,
    In twenty years or more,
And everyone said, "How tall they've grown!
For they've been to the Lakes, and the Torrible Zone,
    And the hills of the Chankly Bore";
And they drank their health, and gave them a feast
Of dumplings made of beautiful yeast;
And everyone said, "If we only live,
We too will go to sea in a Sieve, –
    To the hills of the Chankly Bore!"
      Far and few, far and few,
        Are the lands where the Jumblies live;
       Their heads are green, and their hands are blue,
        And they went to sea in a Sieve.

THE DADDY LONG-LEGS AND THE FLY

Once Mr Daddy Long-legs,
   Dressed in brown and gray,
Walked about upon the sands
   Upon a summer's day;
And there among the pebbles,
   When the wind was rather cold,
He met with Mr Floppy Fly,
   All dressed in blue and gold.
And as it was too soon to dine,
They drank some Periwinkle-wine,
And played an hour or two, or more,
At battlecock and shuttledore.

Said Mr Daddy Long-legs
   To Mr Floppy Fly,
"Why do you never come to court?
   I wish you'd tell me why.
All gold and shine, in dress so fine,
   You'd quite delight the court.
Why do you never go at all?
   I really think you *ought*!
And if you went, you'd see such sights!
Such rugs! and jugs! and candle-lights!
And more than all, the King and Queen,
One in red, and one in green!"

"O Mr Daddy Long-legs,"
   Said Mr Floppy Fly,
"It's true I never go to court,
   And I will tell you why.
If I had six long legs like yours,
   At once I'd go to court!
But oh! I can't, because *my* legs
   Are so extremely short.
And I'm afraid the King and Queen
(One in red, and one in green)
Would say aloud, 'You are not fit,
You Fly, to come to court a bit!' "

"O Mr Daddy Long-legs,"
  Said Mr Floppy Fly,
"I wish you'd sing one little song!
  One mumbian melody!
You used to sing so awful well
  In former days gone by,
But now you never sing at all;
  I wish you'd tell me why:
For if you would, the silvery sound
Would please the shrimps and cockles round,
And all the crabs would gladly come
To hear you sing, 'Ah, Hum di Hum'!"

Said Mr Daddy Long-legs,
  "I can never sing again!
And if you wish, I'll tell you why,
  Although it gives me pain.
For years I cannot hum a bit,
  Or sing the smallest song;
And this the dreadful reason is,
  My legs are grown too long!
My six long legs, all here and there,
Oppress my bosom with despair;
And if I stand, or lie, or sit,
I cannot sing one single bit!"

So Mr Daddy Long-legs
  And Mr Floppy Fly
Sat down in silence by the sea,
  And gazed upon the sky.
They said, "This is a dreadful thing!
The world has all gone wrong,
Since one has legs too short by half,
  The other much too long!
One never more can to go court,
Because his legs have grown too short;
The other cannot sing a song,
Because his legs have grown too long!"

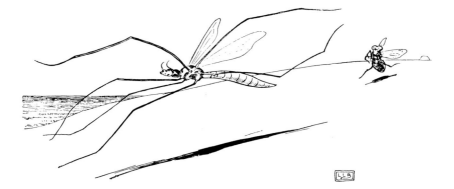

Then Mr Daddy Long-legs
   And Mr Floppy Fly
Rushed downward to the foamy sea
   With one sponge-taneous cry;
And there they found a little boat,
   Whose sails were pink and gray;
And off they sailed among the waves,
   Far, and far away.
They sailed across the silent main,
And reached the great Gromboolian plain;
And there they play for evermore
At battlecock and shuttledore.

The Pelican Chorus

Music by Edward Lear

King and Queen of the Pelicans we;
No other Birds so grand we see!
None but we have feet like fins!
With lovely leathery throats and chins!
   Ploffskin, Pluffskin, Pelican jee!
   We think no Birds so happy as we!
   Plumpskin, Ploshkin, Pelican jill!
   We think so then, and we thought so still!

We live on the Nile. The Nile we love.
By night we sleep on the cliffs above;
By day we fish, and at eve we stand
On long bare islands of yellow sand.
And when the sun sinks slowly down
And the great rock walls grow dark and brown,
Where the purple river rolls fast and dim
And the Ivory Ibis starlike skim,
Wing to wing we dance around, –
Stamping our feet with a flumpy sound, –
Opening our mouths as Pelicans ought,
And this is the song we nightly snort; –
    Ploffskin, Pluffskin, Pelican jee, –
    We think no Birds so happy as we!
    Plumpskin, Ploshkin, Pelican jill, –
    We think so then, and we thought so still!

Last year came out our Daughter, Dell;
And all the Birds received her well.
To do her honour, a feast we made
For every bird that can swim or wade.
Herons and Gulls, and Cormorants black,
Cranes, and Flamingoes with scarlet back,
Plovers and Storks, and Geese in clouds,
Swans and Dilberry Ducks in crowds.
Thousands of Birds in wondrous flight!
They ate and drank and danced all night,
And echoing back from the rocks you heard
Multitude-echoes from Bird and Bird, –

Ploffskin, Pluffskin, Pelican jee,
We think no Birds so happy as we!
Plumpskin, Ploshkin, Pelican jill, –
We think so then, and we thought so still!

Yes, they came; and among the rest,
The King of the Cranes all grandly dressed.
Such a lovely tail! Its feathers float
Between the ends of his blue dress-coat;
With pea-green trowsers all so neat,
And a delicate frill to hide his feet, –
(For though no one speaks of it, everyone knows,
He has got no webs between his toes!)

As soon as he saw our Daughter Dell,
In violent love that Crane King fell, –
On seeing her waddling form so fair,
With a wreath of shrimps in her short white hair.
And before the end of the next long day,
Our Dell had given her heart away;
For the King of the Cranes had won that heart,
With a Crocodile's egg and a large fish-tart.
She vowed to marry the King of the Cranes,
Leaving the Nile for stranger plains;

And away they flew in a gathering crowd
Of endless birds in a lengthening cloud.
 Ploffskin, Pluffskin, Pelican jee, –
 We think no Birds so happy as we!
 Plumpskin, Ploshkin, Pelican jill, –
 We think so then, and we thought so still!

And far away in the twilight sky,
We heard them singing a lessening cry, –
Farther and farther till out of sight,
And we stood alone in the silent night!
Often since, in the nights of June,
We sit on the sand and watch the moon; –

She has gone to the great Gromboolian plain,
And we probably never shall meet again!
Oft, in the long still nights of June,
We sit on the rocks and watch the moon; –
She dwells by the streams of the Chankly Bore,
And we probably never shall see her more.
   Ploffskin, Pluffskin, Pelican jee,
   We think no Birds so happy as we!
   Plumpskin, Ploshkin, Pelican jill, –
   We think so then, and we thought so still!

Said the Duck to the Kangaroo,
    "Good gracious! how you hop!
Over the fields and the water too,
    As if you never would stop!
My life is a bore in this nasty pond,
And I long to go out in the world beyond!

I wish I could hop like you!"
Said the Duck to the Kangaroo.

"Please give me a ride on your back!"
    Said the Duck to the Kangaroo.
"I would sit quite still, and say nothing but 'Quack,'
    The whole of the long day through!
And we'd go to the Dee, and the Jelly Bo Lee,
Over the land, and over the sea; –
    Please take me a ride! O do!"
    Said the Duck to the Kangaroo.

Said the Kangaroo to the Duck,
    "This requires some little reflection;
Perhaps on the whole it might bring me luck,
    And there seems but one objection,
Which is, if you'll let me speak so bold,
Your feet are unpleasantly wet and cold,
And would probably give me the roo-
    Matiz!" said the Kangaroo.

Said the Duck, "As I sate on the rocks,
    I have thought over that completely,
And I bought four pairs of worsted socks
    Which fit my web-feet neatly.
And to keep out the cold I've bought a cloak,
And every day a cigar I'll smoke,
    All to follow my own dear true
    Love of a Kangaroo!"

Said the Kangaroo, "I'm ready!
  All in the moonlight pale;
But to balance me well, dear Duck, sit steady!
  And quite at the end of my tail!"
So away they went with a hop and a bound,
And they hopped the whole world three times round;
  And who so happy, – O who,
  As the Duck and the Kangaroo?

The Broom and the Shovel, the Poker and Tongs,
    They all took a drive in the Park,
And they each sang a song, Ding-a-dong, Ding-a-dong,
    Before they went back in the dark.
Mr Poker he sate quite upright in the coach,
    Mr Tongs made a clatter and clash,
Miss Shovel was dressed all in black (with a brooch),
    Mrs Broom was in blue (with a sash).
        Ding-a-dong! Ding-a-dong!
        And they all sang a song!

"O Shovely so lovely!" the Poker he sang,
    "You have perfectly conquered my heart!
Ding-a-dong! Ding-a-dong! If you're pleased with my song,
    I will feed you with cold apple tart!
When you scrape up the coals with a delicate sound,
    You enrapture my life with delight!
Your nose is so shiny! your head is so round!
    And your shape is so slender and bright!
        Ding-a-dong! Ding-a-dong!
        Ain't you pleased with my song?"

"Alas! Mrs Broom!" sighed the Tongs in his song,
   "O is it because I'm so thin,
And my legs are so long – Ding-a-dong! Ding-a-dong!
   That you don't care about me a pin?
Ah! fairest of creatures, when sweeping the room,
   Ah! why don't you heed my complaint!
Must you needs be so cruel, you beautiful Broom,
   Because you are covered with paint?
      Ding-a-dong! Ding-a-dong!
      You are certainly wrong!"

Mrs Broom and Miss Shovel together they sang,
  "What nonsense you're singing today!"
Said the Shovel, "I'll certainly hit you a bang!"
  Said the Broom, "And I'll sweep you away!"
So the Coachman drove homeward as fast as he could,
  Perceiving their anger with pain;
But they put on the kettle, and little by little,
  They all became happy again.
        Ding-a-dong! Ding-a-dong!
        There's an end of my song!

There lived an Old Man in the Kingdom of Tess,
Who invented a purely original dress;
And when it was perfectly made and complete,
He opened the door, and walked into the street.

By way of a hat, he'd a loaf of Brown Bread,
In the middle of which he inserted his head; –
His Shirt was made up of no end of dead Mice,
The warmth of whose skins was quite fluffy and nice; –
His Drawers were of Rabbit-skins; – so were his Shoes; –
His Stockings were skins, – but it is not known whose; –
His Waistcoat and Trowsers were made of Pork Chops; –
His Buttons were Jujubes, and Chocolate Drops; –
His Coat was all Pancakes with Jam for a border,
And a girdle of Biscuits to keep it in order;
And he wore over all, as a screen from bad weather,
A Cloak of green Cabbage-leaves stitched all together.

He had walked a short way, when he heard a great noise,
Of all sorts of Beasticles, Birdlings, and Boys; –
And from every long street and dark lane in the town
Beasts, Birdles, and Boys in a tumult rushed down.
Two Cows and a Calf ate his Cabbage-leaf Cloak; –
Four Apes seized his Girdle, which vanished like smoke; –
Three Kids ate up half of his Pancakey Coat, –
And the tails were devour'd by an ancient He-Goat; –
An army of Dogs in a twinkling tore *up* his
Pork Waistcoat and Trowsers to give to their Puppies; –
And while they were growling, and mumbling the Chops,
Ten Boys prigged the Jujubes and Chocolate Drops. –

He tried to run back to his house, but in vain,
For Scores of fat Pigs came again and again; –
They rushed out of stables and hovels and doors, –
They tore off his stockings, his shoes, and his drawers; –
And now from the housetops with screechings descend,
Striped, spotted, white, black, and grey Cats without end,
They jumped on his shoulders and knocked off his hat, –
When Crows, Ducks, and Hens made a mincemeat of that; –
They speedily flew at his sleeves in a trice,
And utterly tore up his Shirt of dead Mice; –
They swallowed the last of his Shirt with a squall, –
Whereon he ran home with no clothes on at all.

And he said to himself as he bolted the door,
"I will not wear a similar dress any more,
Any more, any more, any more, never more!"

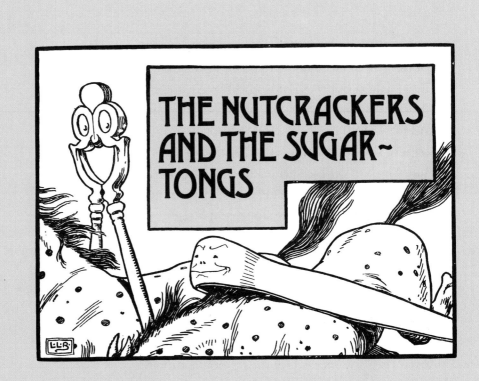

The Nutcrackers sate by a plate on the table,
  The Sugar-tongs sate by a plate at his side;
And the Nutcrackers said, "Don't you wish we were able
  Along the blue hills and green meadows to ride?
Must we drag on this stupid existence for ever,
  So idle and weary, so full of remorse, –
While everyone else takes his pleasure, and never
  Seems happy unless he is riding a horse?"

"Don't you think we could ride without being instructed?
  Without any saddle, or bridle, or spur?
Our legs are so long, and so aptly constructed,
  I'm sure that an accident could not occur.
Let us all of a sudden hop down from the table,
  And hustle downstairs, and each jump on a horse!
Shall we try? Shall we go? Do you think we are able?"
  The Sugar-tongs answered distinctly, "Of course!"

So down the long staircase they hopped in a minute,
    The Sugar-tongs snapped, and the Crackers said, "Crack!"
The stable was open, the horses were in it;
    Each took out a pony, and jumped on his back.
The Cat in a fright scrambled out of the doorway,
    The Mice tumbled out of a bundle of hay,
The brown and white Rats, and the black ones from Norway,
    Screamed out, "They are taking the horses away!"

The whole of the household was filled with amazement,
    The Cups and the Saucers danced madly about,
The Plates and the Dishes looked out of the casement,
    The Saltcellar stood on his head with a shout,
The Spoons with a clatter looked out of the lattice,
    The Mustard-pot climbed up the Gooseberry Pies,
The Soup-ladle peeped through a heap of Veal Patties,
    And squeaked with a ladle-like scream of surprise.

The Frying-pan said, "It's an awful delusion!"
   The Tea-kettle hissed and grew black in the face;
And they all rushed downstairs in the wildest confusion,
   To see the great Nutcracker-Sugar-tong race.
And out of the stable, with screamings and laughter
   (Their ponies were cream-coloured, speckled with brown)
The Nutcrackers first, and the Sugar-tongs after,
   Rode all around the yard, and then all round the town.

They rode through the street, and they rode by the station,
    They galloped away to the beautiful shore;
In silence they rode, and "made no observation",
    Save this: "We will never go back any more!"
And still you might hear, till they rode out of hearing,
    The Sugar-tongs snap, and the Crackers say, "Crack!"
Till far in the distance their forms disapppearing,
    They faded away. – And they never came back!

Said the Table to the Chair,
"You can hardly be aware,
How I suffer from the heat,
And from chilblains on my feet!
If we took a little walk,
We might have a little talk!
Pray let us take the air!"
Said the Table to the Chair.

Said the Chair unto the Table,
"Now you *know* we are not able!
How foolishly you talk,
When you know we *cannot* walk!"
Said the Table, with a sigh,
"It can do no harm to try,
I've as many legs as you,
Why can't we walk on two?"

So they both went slowly down,
And walked about the town
With a cheerful bumpy sound,
As they toddled round and round.
And everybody cried,
As they hastened to their side,
"See! The Table and the Chair
Have come out to take the air!"

But in going down an alley,
To a castle in a valley,
They completely lost their way,
And wandered all the day,
Till, to see them safely back,
They paid a Ducky-quack,
And a Beetle, and a Mouse,
Who took them to their house.

Then they whispered to each other,
"O delightful little brother!
What a lovely walk we've taken!
Let us dine on Beans and Bacon!"
So the Ducky, and the leetle
Browny-Mousy and the Beetle
Dined, and danced upon their heads
Till they toddled to their beds.

Mr and Mrs Discobbolos
    Climbed to the top of a wall
  And they sate to watch the sunset sky
  And to hear the Nupiter Piffkin cry
    And the Biscuit Buffalo call.
They took up a roll and some Camomile tea,
And both were as happy as happy could be –
    Till Mrs Discobbolos said, –
    "Oh! W! X! Y! Z!
    It has just come into my head –
Suppose we should happen to fall! ! ! ! !
      Darling Mr Discobbolos"

"Suppose we should fall down flumpetty
     Just like pieces of stone!
   On to the thorns, – or into the moat!
   What would become of your new green coat
     And might you not break a bone?
It never occurred to me before –
That perhaps we shall never go down any more!"
        And Mrs Discobbolos said –
        "Oh! W! X! Y! Z!
        What put it into your head
   To climb up this wall? – my own
              Darling Mr Discobbolos?"

Mr Discobbolos answered, –
     "At first it gave me pain, –
   And I felt my ears turn perfectly pink
   When your exclamation made me think
     We might never get down again!
But now I believe it is wiser far
To remain for ever just where we are." –

And Mr Discobbolos said,
   "Oh! W! X! Y! Z!
    It has just come into my head –
– We shall never go down again –
      Dearest Mrs Discobbolos!"

So Mr and Mrs Discobbolos
  Stood up, and began to sing,
 "Far away from hurry and strife
Here we will pass the rest of life,
  Ding a dong, ding, dong, ding!
We want no knives nor forks nor chairs,
No tables nor carpets nor household cares,
   From worry of life we've fled –
   Oh! W! X! Y! Z!
   There is no more trouble ahead,
 Sorrow or any such thing –
    For Mr and Mrs Discobbolos!"

O my aged Uncle Arly!
Sitting on a heap of Barley
    Thro' the silent hours of night, –
Close beside a leafy thicket: –
On his nose there was a Cricket, –
In his hat a Railway-Ticket; –
    (But his shoes were far too tight).

Long ago, in youth, he squander'd
All his goods away, and wander'd
    To the Tiniskoop-hills afar.
There on golden sunsets blazing,
Every evening found him gazing, –
Singing, – "Orb! You're quite amazing!
    How I wonder what you are!"

Like the ancient Medes and Persians,
Always by his own exertions
    He subsisted on those hills; –
Whiles, – by teaching children spelling, –
Or at times by merely yelling, –
Or at intervals by selling
    Propter's Nicodemus Pills.

Later, in his morning rambles
He perceived the moving brambles –
    Something square and white disclose; –
'Twas a First-class Railway-Ticket;
But, on stooping down to pick it
Off the ground, – a pea-green Cricket
    Settled on my uncle's Nose.

Never – never more, – oh! never,
Did that Cricket leave him ever,–
    Dawn or evening, day or night; –
Clinging as a constant treasure, –
Chirping with a cheerious measure, –
Wholly to my uncle's pleasure, –
    (Though his shoes were far too tight).

So for three-and-forty winters,
Till his shoes were worn to splinters,
    All those hills he wander'd o'er, –
Sometimes silent; – sometimes yelling; –
Till he came to Borley-Melling,
Near his old ancestral dwelling; –
    (But his shoes were far too tight).

BORLEY-MELLING
ONE MILE

On a little heap of Barley
Died my aged Uncle Arly,
    And they buried him one night; –
Close beside the leafy thicket; –
There, – his hat and Railway-Ticket; –
There, – his ever-faithful Cricket; –
    (But his shoes were far too tight).

Two old Bachelors were living in one house;
One caught a Muffin, the other caught a Mouse.
Said he who caught the Muffin to him who caught the Mouse, –
"This happens just in time! For we've nothing in the house,
Save a tiny slice of lemon and a teaspoonful of honey,
And what to do for dinner – since we haven't any money?
And what can we expect if we haven't any dinner,
But to lose our teeth and eyelashes and keep on growing thinner?"

Said he who caught the Mouse to him who caught the Muffin, –
"We might cook this little Mouse, if we only had some Stuffin'!
If we had but Sage and Onion we could do extremely well,
But how to get that Stuffin' it is difficult to tell" –
Those two old Bachelors ran quickly to the town
And asked for Sage and Onions as they wandered up and down;
They borrowed two large Onions, but no Sage was to be found
In the Shops, or in the Market, or in all the Gardens round.

But someone said – "A hill there is, a little to the north,
And to its purpledicular top a narrow way leads forth; –
And there among the rugged rocks abides an ancient Sage, –
An earnest Man, who reads all day a most perplexing page.
Climb up, and seize him by the toes! – all studious as he sits, –
And pull him down, – and chop him into endless little bits!
Then mix him with your Onion (cut up likewise into Scraps) –
When your Stuffin' will be ready – and very good: perhaps."

Those two old Bachelors without loss of time
The nearly purpledicular crags at once began to climb;
And at the top, among the rocks, all seated in a nook,
They saw that Sage, a-reading of a most enormous book.
"You earnest Sage!" aloud they cried, "your book you've read enough in! –
We wish to chop you into bits to mix you into Stuffin'!" –

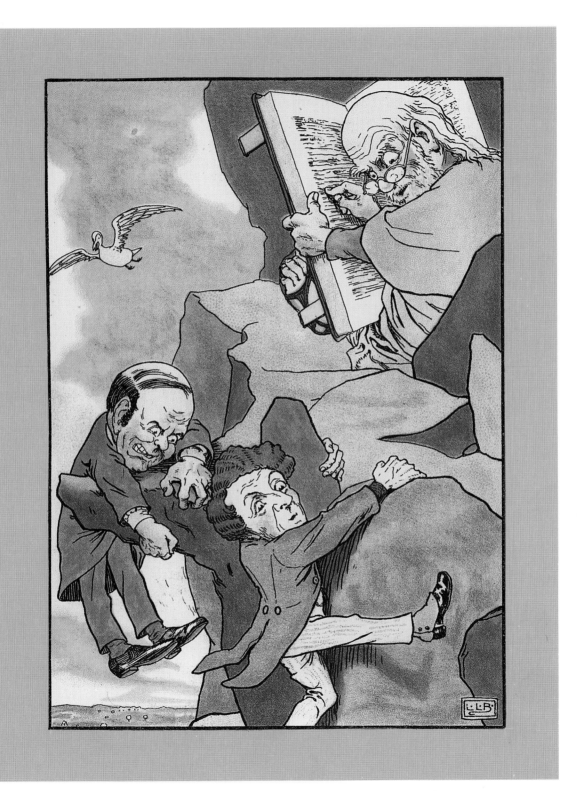

But that old Sage looked calmy up, and with his awful book,
At those two Bachelors' bald heads a certain aim he took; –
And over Crag and precipice they rolled promiscuous down, –
At once they rolled, and never stopped in lane or field or town, –
And when they reached their house, they found
   (besides their want of Stuffin')
The Mouse had fled; – and, previously, had eaten up the Muffin.

They left their home in silence by the once convivial door.
And from that hour those Bachelors were never heard of more.

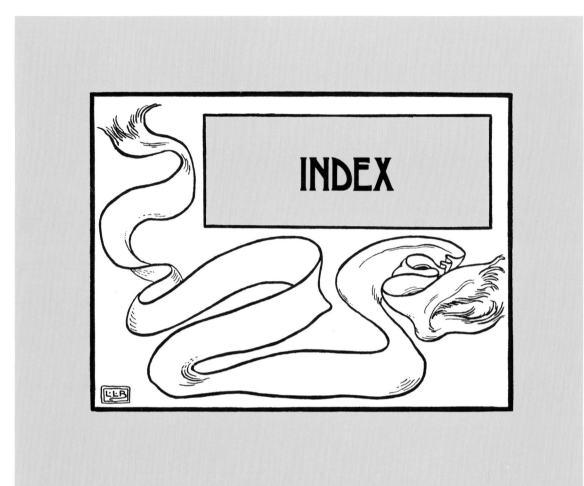

INDEX

Titles are in *italics*. Where the title and the first line are the same,
the first line only is listed.